EDGE BOOKS™

HORSES

The FRIESIAN Horse

by Lori Coleman

Consultant:
Laurie Kasperek
Editorial Committee
The Friesian Magazine

Capstone *press*

Mankato, Minnesota

Edge Books are published by Capstone Press,
151 Good Counsel Drive, P.O. Box 669, Mankato, Minnesota 56002.
www.capstonepress.com

Library of Congress Cataloging-in-Publication Data
Coleman, Lori.
    The Friesian horse / by Lori Coleman.
    p. cm.—(Edge Books. Horses)
    Summary: "Describes Friesian horses, including their history, physical
features, and primary uses"—Provided by publisher.
    Includes bibliographical references and index.
    ISBN-13: 978-0-7368-5825-0 (hardcover)
    ISBN-10: 0-7368-5825-3 (hardcover)
    1. Friesian horse—Juvenile literature. I. Title. II. Series.
SF293.F9C65 2006
636.1'3—dc22   2005019426

Editorial Credits
Angie Kaelberer, editor; Juliette Peters, set designer; Bobbi J. Dey, book designer;
    Deirdre Barton, photo researcher/photo editor

Photo Credits
Front cover, back cover, and all interior photos except page 26 by
    Gloria Muscarella/Cheval Photography
Capstone Press/Karon Dubke, 26

1 2 3 4 5 6 11 10 09 08 07 06

Table of Contents

FEATURES

Chapter 1

Horses of the Knights

During the Middle Ages (400–1500), the clanging of metal and the loud clip-clop of horses' hooves rang through the thick forests of northern Europe. Knights in suits of armor carried weapons as they rode big, strong horses from battle to battle. Many of these horses came from Friesland.

Friesland is part of the Netherlands. The Frisian people have lived in this area since about 500 BC. The ancient Frisians were known for raising and trading horses and cattle. The horses they bred are now called Friesians.

Learn about:
- ★ **First Friesians**
- ★ **Uses**
- ★ **Registries**

Today, people dressed as knights ride Friesians in jousting contests.

Changes in the Breed

The Renaissance (1400–1600) followed the Middle Ages. People placed more value on art and beauty. They wanted thinner, more elegant horses. Breeders mated Friesians with Spanish Andalusians. Today's Friesians owe their high step and arched necks to Andalusians.

A sjees has two large wheels and room for a driver and one passenger.

American Friesians

In the 1600s, Dutch people brought Friesian horses to North America. The Friesians were bred with other horses. Purebred Friesians disappeared in the United States. The breed didn't return until 300 years later.

Owners brought Friesians to classical riding schools in Spain, France, and Austria. The classical riding style later developed into modern dressage. In dressage competitions, horses and riders perform a series of advanced movements.

A Useful Horse

During the 1700s, Friesian horses had a variety of jobs. They did farmwork, raced, and pulled carriages.

In the Netherlands, a small two-person carriage called a sjees was in style. The carriage was covered with carvings and finely painted decorations in gold and silver. One or more Friesians were often seen pulling the sjezen.

About 45,000 Friesians are registered with the Studbook Society.

A Rocky Time

By the 1800s, Friesians had fallen out of favor with many people. Horse racers were turning to Thoroughbreds, which were faster than Friesians. Larger, heavier draft horses were taking over fieldwork. The number of purebred Friesians dwindled.

In 1879, a group of Friesian owners in the Netherlands decided to save the breed. They started the Studbook Society to register Friesians. In 1896, members divided the registry into two books. One was for purebred horses bred and kept in Friesland. The other was for horses that were part Friesian. The registries are now combined into the *Friesian Horse Studbook*.

New Beginnings

In the 1970s, breeders Thomas Hannon and Frank Leyendekker brought Friesians to the United States from the Netherlands. Leyendekker later helped start the Friesian Horse Association of North America (FHANA). This group is a branch of the Studbook Society. About 4,000 North American Friesians are registered with FHANA.

Chapter 2

Black Beauties

With their shiny black coats and flowing manes and tails, Friesians stand out in a crowd. The big, proud horses are calm even in new places and around people they don't know.

Basic Features

Almost all Friesians are black. They range from jet black to black-brown. Sun can fade their coats to a lighter shade.

Friesians' thick manes and tails quickly grow long. Some even touch the ground. Friesians also have long hair called feather on the back of their lower legs.

Learn about:
- ★ **Color**
- ★ **Personality**
- ★ **Names**

Some Friesians' silky manes nearly reach the ground.

Friesians look powerful, and they are. Most weigh at least 1,300 pounds (590 kilograms). Their muscular hindquarters and strong legs move them forward at a forceful pace.

Friesians look proud as they trot. They arch their necks and carry their heads high. The tips of their small ears prick inward.

The name of a Friesian foal must begin with a certain letter.

Registering a Friesian

The Studbook Society sets the rules for registered Friesians. A registered Friesian can have a white spot between its eyes, but no other markings. Breeding stallions must be at least 15.3 hands at the withers, or top of the shoulders. A hand equals about 4 inches (10 centimeters). Registered mares must stand at least 14.3 hands high.

Each year, the Studbook Society picks several letters of the alphabet for naming purposes. Names of all Friesian foals registered that year have to begin with one of these letters. For example, the names of 2005 foals had to begin with P, Q, R, or S. Of course, the foal's owners can call it any name they choose at home.

Full tail

Wide back

Powerful hindquarters

Feather

Long, flowing mane

Small ears

Arched neck

Long, sloping shoulders

15

Chapter 3

Amazing Dancers

The beauty, grace, and intelligence of Friesians make them naturally suited for dressage competitions. Friesians compete at all levels of this crowd-pleasing sport.

Dressage Patterns

Dressage competitions include pattern tests. The horse moves to and from set points in the arena at different gaits, such as the walk, trot, or canter. The arena is marked with letters around the rail. The horse might be expected to trot from A to F, canter to C, stop, and then walk to K.

Learn about:
- ★ Pattern tests
- ★ Gaits
- ★ Freestyle moves

Signs marked with letters guide horses and riders during dressage pattern tests.

As Friesians pass pattern tests, they move up to higher levels. The patterns at these levels include more difficult gaits, such as the countercanter.

When a horse canters, one front leg extends past the other. If the extended leg is the right leg, the horse is on the right lead. It moves around the arena clockwise. If it is the left leg, the horse is on the left lead and moves counterclockwise. Countercantering is when a horse on the left lead moves clockwise or a horse on the right lead moves counterclockwise.

The side-pass is another advanced dressage move. During this move, the horse steps directly to the side. The rider uses the leg, reins, and seat to guide the horse in the right direction.

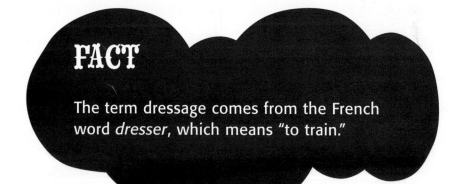

FACT

The term dressage comes from the French word *dresser*, which means "to train."

The side-pass is part of many dressage competitions.

Dancing to Music

Freestyle dressage routines are set to music. Horses almost appear to be dancing as they perform moves such as the piaffe and pirouette. During a piaffe, the horse trots in place. In a pirouette, the horse moves in a circle while keeping its back feet in one place.

Riders and horses train for years to reach the highest dressage levels.

In the highest level of dressage, horses perform airs above the ground. For a levade, the horse stands on its hind legs as its front legs bend slightly. A capriole is one of the most amazing airs above the ground. The horse leaps into the air while extending its back legs.

The Friesian's powerful back legs help it perform the levade.

Training

Training a horse for dressage takes time. Horses and trainers practice between three and six times each week.

For dressage, horses learn to perform each gait in collected, working, and extended forms. In a collected trot, the horse has short strides and is working off the hind legs. A working trot has a slightly longer stride. At an extended trot, the horse reaches out farther with the front legs, creating an even bigger stride.

Chapter 4

Friesians in Action

At parades, people line the streets to watch the high, light steps of Friesians as they pull carriages. Friesians' strength and calmness make them especially good for driving.

Driving Champions

Friesians show off their driving skills at competitions as well as in parades. Many Friesians are driven four-in-hand. The driver controls four horses at once.

Sjezen are still a big part of Friesian horse shows. Drivers and their partners wear traditional clothes, and the carriages are as fancy as in the days of old.

Learn about:
- ★ **Driving**
- ★ **Circuses**
- ★ **Shows**

Driving four-in-hand takes practice and skill.

During tandem driving training, the trainer rides one horse. The trainer uses voice commands, the reins, and a whip to control the other horse.

Friesians do well at tandem driving. Two horses pull the carriage with one in front of the other, instead of side by side.

The quadrille is often the last event at a Friesian show. People stay just to see this spectacular sight. Drivers and passengers in eight sjezen perform together. The horses look like a military drill team as they perform their routines to music.

Circus Performers

Friesians have also earned fame under the big top of circuses. In circuses, Friesian stallions often perform at liberty. During these events, a trainer leads a group of stallions in a ring. The Friesians march together in formation, taking their cues only from the trainer's hand movements.

Major Shows

The largest Friesian show in the United States is the Friesian Extravaganza. It includes classes ranging from Western pleasure to dressage to driving.

The highlight of the Extravaganza is Friesians on Stage. During this event, people dressed as knights in armor ride Friesians into mock battles. Quadrille teams step in perfect time around the ring. Drivers control teams pulling sjezen, chariots, and other types of carriages.

Every year, the International Friesian Show Horse Association (IFSHA) holds the Grand National event. Dressage, driving, and parades are all part of this competition.

Owning a Friesian

The Friesian horse is known both as a competitive horse and as a family friend. Dressage and driving are the Friesians' specialties, but the proud black horses can do just about anything a horse owner

could want. Because Friesians are gentle, kind, and willing, both beginning and experienced riders can do well with them.

The Friesian's history has been troubled at times. But the big black horses have overcome these troubles to become one of the fastest-growing breeds in the world. In the future, horse fans look forward to seeing much more of this elegant breed.

Fast Facts: The Friesian Horse

Name: The Friesian was first bred in Friesland, which is now part of the Netherlands.

History: In Europe, knights rode Friesians during the Middle Ages. Later, Friesians were used for racing, farmwork, and dressage. The breed didn't become well known in North America until the 1970s.

Height: Friesians are 15 to 17 hands (about 5.5 feet or 1.7 meters) tall at the withers. Each hand equals 4 inches (10 centimeters).

Weight: about 1,300 pounds (590 kilograms)

Color: almost always black

Features: thick, muscular bodies; wide backs; arched necks; long, flowing manes and tails; feather on the back of the legs; small, pricked ears

Personality: gentle, calm, cooperative

Abilities: Friesians are generally used for dressage or driving.

Life span: 20 to 25 years

Glossary

capriole (KA-pree-ole)—a dressage move in which a horse leaps into the air while extending its back legs

dressage (druh-SAHJ)—a riding style in which horses complete patterns while doing advanced moves

levade (leh-VAHD)—a rearing move performed in dressage

piaffe (pee-AHF)—a dressage move in which the horse trots in place

pirouette (puhr-uh-WET)—a dressage move in which a horse moves in a circle while keeping its back feet in the same place

quadrille (kwah-DRIL)—a performance involving several horses doing routines to music

sjees (SHAY)—a traditional Dutch carriage for two people; sjezen are more than one sjees.

stallion (STAL-yuhn)—an adult male horse that can be used for breeding

Read More

Beeman, Laura. *The Friesian Horse.* West Conshohocken, Penn.: Infinity Publishing, 2001.

Bolté, Betty. *Dressage.* The Horse Library. Philadelphia: Chelsea House, 2002.

Ransford, Sandy. *Horse & Pony Breeds.* Kingfisher Riding Club. Boston: Kingfisher, 2003.

Internet Sites

FactHound offers a safe, fun way to find Internet sites related to this book. All of the sites on FactHound have been researched by our staff.

Here's how:

1. Visit *www.facthound.com*
2. Type in this special code **0736858253** for age-appropriate sites. Or enter a search word related to this book for a more general search.
3. Click on the **Fetch It** button.

FactHound will fetch the best sites for you!

Index